TENNESSEE VOICES ANTHOLOGY
2019-2020

THE POETRY SOCIETY OF TENNESSEE (PST)

A Member of the National Federation
of State Poetry Societies (NFSPS)

Editorial Board
Matthew Gilbert
Rose Klix
Janet Qually
Pamela Watson

The Poetry Society of Tennessee

Copyright © 2020 The Poetry Society of Tennessee

All rights reserved. No part of this publication may be reproduced, distributed, or transmitted in any form or by any means, including photocopying, recording, or other electronic or mechanical methods, without the prior written permission of the publisher, except in the case of brief quotations embodied in critical reviews and certain other noncommercial uses permitted by copyright law.

ISBN-978-1-951300-11-1

www.poetrytennessee.org

Cover art is from an original painting by William Hill.

Published by Liberation's Publishing LLC

IN MEMORIAM

This issue of Tennessee Voices is
dedicated to the memory of

Margaret Burton McCarty
August 23, 1921–November 11, 2017

an original founding member in 1953
who prepared the original charter,
and in 1976-77 was selected as
an Honorary Member of
The Poetry Society of Tennessee

and

Jeanine Edwards Mah
August 26, 1931–December 17, 2019

a Member of
The Poetry Society of Tennessee and
selected as the society's Poet Laureate 2011-12

STARLIGHT

The sky is filled with stars tonight
as I sit and think of when we met,
a time when both our futures were bright,
a time to love, one never to regret.
I still see your face
and feel your touch;
I hear your laughter and
remember your grace.
You left too soon and went alone
leaving only memories for me to hold.
But in empty rooms I find you still and
the sky is filled with stars tonight.

JEANINE MAH, Memphis, TN

Her poem was previously published in the 2010-2011 *Tennessee Voices* Anthology as the 1st place winner of The Frieda B. Dorris Memorial Contest.

CONTENTS

PST Officers and Committees 6

The History of The Poetry Society of Tenneessee 14

PST Poets Laureate 15

PST Honorary Members 16

Winners of Annual and Monthly Contests 18

The 2019 Mid-South Poetry Festival 33

Winners of the Festival Poems 36

Student Winners 75

The Eye Poem 80

Patron Poems 83

Index of First Place Winners 100

POETRY SOCIETY OF TENNESSEE (PST) OFFICERS AND COMMITTEE CHAIRPERSONS

PST OFFICERS 2019-2020

President: JoAn Howerton
Vice President: Russell H. Strauss
Corresponding Secretary: Lori Goetz
Treasurer: Janet Qually
Director: Florence Bruce
Director: William Hill
Parliamentarian: Frances Cowden

PST COMMITTEE CHAIRPERSONS 2019-2020
Monthly Contest Coordinator: Ann Carolyn Cates
Website: Lori Goetz
Program Chairpersons:
Florence Bruce/Lori Goetz/JoAn Howerton/Russell Strauss
Student Contest Coordinator: Frances Cowden

63ʳᴰ ANNUAL MID-SOUTH POETRY FESTIVAL
(2019)
Festival Director: JoAn Howerton
Contest Coordinator: Lori Goetz
Assistants to Festival Director:
Janet Qually/William Hill

PST OFFICERS 2020-2021

President: Lori Goetz
Vice President: William Hill
Corresponding Secretary: Elizabeth Shelley
Treasurer: Janet Qually
Director: Russell H. Strauss
Director: Ann Carolyn Cates

PST COMMITTEE CHAIRPERSONS 2020-2021

Monthly Contest Coordinator: Ann Carolyn Cates
Website: Lori Goetz
Program Chairpersons: TBD
Student Contest Coordinator: Frances Cowden

64TH ANNUAL MID-SOUTH POETRY FESTIVAL (2020)

Festival Director/Contest Chair: Lori Goetz
Assistants to Festival Director:
TBD

CHAPTERS AFFILIATED WITH THE POETRY SOCIETY OF TENNESSEE (PST)

PST-WEST TENNESSEE

PST was founded in Memphis in 1953 as the only state chapter prior to 2010. In 2019, PST-West was formed to include local activities and to distinguish the state society functions from the local chapter activities. West designates it is inclusive of areas in and outside Memphis. For current meeting information see https://www.poetrytennessee.org/

PST-NORTHEAST TENNESSEE (PST-NE)

In 2010, PST-NE was founded in Gray, TN. In 2018, the chapter meetings were moved to Johnson City, TN. Northeast designates that they are inclusive of areas in and around the Tri-Cities. For current meeting information see http://pstne.weebly.com/

PST-KNOXVILLE, TENNESSEE

PST- Knoxville was founded in 2017. Meetings and activities focus on the Knoxville area. For current meeting information see https://www.facebook.com/PSTKnox/

PST-MIDDLE TENNESSEE

This is a proposed chapter to be founded from Members-at-Large in the Middle Tennessee area once sufficient members join.

The Poetry Society of Tennessee

PST-WEST OFFICERS AND COMMITTEE CHAIRPERSONS 2019-2020

Currently the same as PST

PST-NE OFFICERS AND COMMITTEE CHAIRPERSONS 2019-2020

President: Rose Klix
Vice President: Calvin Ross
Treasurer/Membership: Howard S. Carman, Jr.
Secretaries: Jan Barnett and Connie Mohr
Webmaster: J. Michael Ramey
Facebook: Howard S. Carman, Jr.
Newsletter/Publicity: Judith Donley
PST-NE Contest Coordinator: Carolyn Lilly
Critique Meeting Coordinators:
Rose Klix/Calvin Ross/Ben Weakley

PST-KNOXVILLE OFFICERS 2019-2020

President: Sharon Mishler Fox
Vice President: Ann Thornfield Long
Secretary/Treasurer: Kay Fields

PST-MIDDLE TENNESSEE OFFICERS

(TBD)

PST-WEST OFFICERS AND COMMITTEE CHAIRPERSONS 2020-2021

Currently the same as PST

PST-NE OFFICERS AND COMMITTEE CHAIRPERSONS 2020-2021

President: Calvin Ross
Vice President for Programs: Jerry Buchanan
Vice President for Communications: Lisa Kamolnick
Treasurer/Membership: Howard S. Carman, Jr.
Secretary: Margaret LoBue
Webmaster: J. Michael Ramey
Facebook: Lisa Kamolnick
Newsletter/Publicity: Matthew Gilbert
PST Liaison: Rose Klix
PST-NE Contest Coordinator: Rose Klix
Critique Meeting Coordinators:
Howard S. Carmon, Jr./Calvin Ross/Ben Weakley

PST-KNOXVILLE OFFICERS 2020-2021

President: Sharon Mishler Fox Sweeney
Vice President: Ann Thornfield Long
Secretary/Treasurer: Kay Fields

PST-MIDDLE TENNESSEE OFFICERS

(TBD)

RECORD OF PST/PST-WEST PAST PRESIDENTS

Raymond McCarty	1953-1954
Charlie W. Sturm	1954-1955
Gordon Lockhart	1955-1956
Louise Malone Ross	1956-1957
Ann Gordon Dean	1957-1958
Walter Chandler	1958-1959
Lillian Terry Harrison	1959-1960
Anna Gordon Dean	1960-1961
Patricia Murphy Reber	1961-1962
Walter Chandler	1962-1963
Gordon Lockhart	1963-1965
Lucille D. Short	1965-1966
J. Pat Babin	1966-1968
Robert Simonton	1968-1970
Frieda Beasley Dorris	1970-1972
Dr. Rosemary Stephens	1972-1974
Bee Bacherig Long	1974-1976
Ann Carolyn Cates	1976-1977
Jerry Leo Robbins	1977-1979
Chester A. Rider	1979-1981
Kenneth D. Thomas	1981-1983
Dr. Wanda A. Rider	1983-1984
Robert Simonton	1984-1985
Elizabeth Pell	1985-1986
Lula May Adams	1986-1987
Frances Brinkley Cowden	1987-1989
Thomas McDaniel	1989-1990
La Nita Crouch Moses	1990-1991
Ann Carolyn Cates	1991-1992
Ruth Thomas	1992-1993
D. Beecher Smith, II	1993-1995
Dr. Diane M. Clark	1995-1997
Patricia Smith	1997-1999
Russell H. Strauss	1999-2001

Frances Brinkley Cowden	2001-2002
Nellie H. Jones	2002-2003
Michael R. Denington	2003-2005
Russell H. Strauss	2005-2007
Michael R. Dennington	2007-2008
Russell H. Strauss	2008-2010
Sarah Hull Gurley	2010-2011
Randall Stoker	2011-2013
JoAn Howerton	2013-2015
Russell H. Strauss	2015-2017
Leslie Blakeburn	2017-2018
JoAn Howerton	2018-2020

PST-NE PAST PRESIDENTS

This chapter was founded on February 13, 2010.

Rose Klix	2010-2013
Co-Presidents:	2013-2014
Hugh Webb and Chrissie Anderson Peters	
Todd Bailey	2014-2015
J. Michael Ramey	2015-2016
Gretchen McCroskey	2016-2018
Rose Klix	2018-2020

PST-KNOXVILLE PAST PRESIDENT

This chapter was founded on August 30, 2017.

Sharon Mishler Fox Sweeney	2017-2020

THE HISTORY OF THE POETRY SOCIETY OF TENNESSEE (PST)

Charter of Incorporation: The Charter of The Poetry Society of Tennessee was granted June 30, 1953. Prepared by Margaret B. McCarty, Charter Member.

Founders: The seven signers of the charter are the founding members. At the second general meeting on June 20, 1953, these members were elected as the first officers of the new organization. Their names and offices are as follows:
President: Raymond McCarty
Vice President: Charlie W. Sturm
Recording Secretary: Inez E. Andersen
Corresponding Secretary: Cleo John Fox
Treasurer: Margaret B. McCarty
Directors: Kenneth L. Beaudoin and Gordon Lockhart

Purpose: According to the Society Charter, the organization was constituted "for the purpose of bringing into being a close comradeship and mutual working fellowship among the recognized poets of the state; stimulating the as yet unrecognized poets of the state to make an effort for recognition in the established channels of expression; sponsoring the recognition of poetry as a creative art in the educational institutions within this state by encouraging the youth of Tennessee to secure the cultural background and appreciation necessary to achieve stature as a poet; and assisting and encouraging in every way possible the development of creative talent in the field of poetry."

Meetings: Regular meetings have been at 2 p.m. on the first Saturday of each month excluding summer months (June, July, August), and October (Mid-South Poetry Festival). Since January 2013, the meetings have been held at the White Station Public Library, Memphis, TN.

PST POETS LAUREATE

Inez Elliott Andersen	1975-1976
Charles Stanfill	1976-1977
Raymond McCarty	1977-1978
Eve Braden Hatchett	1978-1979
Robert Simonton	1978-1979
Frieda Beasley Dorris	1979-1980
Bee Bacherig Long	1980-1981
Chester G. Rider	1981-1982
Kenneth L. Beaudoin	1982-1983
Kenneth Thomas	1983-1984
Mildred Boydton	1984-1985
Carrie Sharpe	1985-1986
Ann Carolyn Cates	1986-1987
La Nita Moses	1987-1988
Dr. Malra Treece	1988-1989
Frances Brinkley Cowden	1989-1990
Isabel Joshlin Glaser	1990-1991
Thomas McDaniel	1991-1992
Helen Allison	1992-1993
Lucille Byrd Pitchford	1993-1994
Norma W. Young	1994-1995
D. Beecher Smith, II	1995-1996
Louise Gearin	1996-1997
Dr. Diane M. Clark	1997-1998
Dr. Rosemary Stephens	1998-1999
Patricia W. Smith	1999-2000
Nellie Jones	2000-2001
Russell H. Strauss	2001-2002
Florence Bruce	2002-2003
Harold Baldwin	2004-2005
Michael R. Denington	2005-2006
Malu Graham	2006-2007
Elizabeth Pell	2007-2008
J. Pompford Harris	2008-2009

Sara Hull Gurley	2009-2010
Angela Logsdon	2010-2011
Rose Klix	2010-2011
Jeanine Mah	2011-2012
Leslie Blakeburn	2012-2013
Caroline Sposto	2013-2014
Randall Stoker	2014-2015
Llewellyn Brawner	2015-2016
Prince McLemore	2016-2017
Charles K. Firmage	2017-2018
Janet Qually	2018-2019
Lori Goetz	2019-2020
Gretchen McCroskey	2020-2021

PST HONORARY MEMBERS

Florence Cogburn LeCoq	1955-1956
Nora Johnson Cantrell	1955-1956
Robert Sparks Walker	1959-1960
Jane Merchant	1960-1961
Paul Flowers	1962-1963
Ollie Barnes Dayton	1964-1965
Clarice Riddley Kelso	1964-1965
Gordon Lockhart	1965-1967
Inez Elliot Andersen	1972-1973
Kenneth Lawrence Beaudoin	1972-1973
Charlie Weddle Strum	1975-1976
Margaret B. McCarty	1976-1977
Raymond McCarty	1976-1977
Ercil F. Brown	1983-1984
Claudia Watson Stewart	1983-1984
Margaret Gordon Williamson	1983-1984
Bee Bacherig Long	1984-1985
Lucille D. Short	1985-1986
Frieda Beasley Dorris	1988-1989

Eve Braden Hatchett	1988-1989
Corinne Frierson Hughes	1988-1989
Helen Thomas Allison	1991-1992
Robert Simonton	1994-1995
Dr. Rosemary Stephens	1994-1995
Kenneth D. Thomas	1994-1995
Lorraine Smith	1997-1998
Dr. Malra Treece	1999-2000
*Frances Brinkley Cowden	1999-2000
*Thomas McDaniel	1999-2000
*Dr. Diane M. Clark	1999-2000
Patricia W. Smith	2004-2005
Michael R. Denington	2008-2009
*Ann Carolyn Cates	2010-2011
*Elizabeth Pell	2010-2011
*Russell H. Strauss	2011-2012
*Randall Stoker	2011-2012
*J. Pompford Harris	2011-2012
*Florence Bruce	2015-2016
*Sarah Hull Gurley	2015-2016

**Current Honorary Members*

WINNERS OF PST MEMBERS-ONLY ANNUAL SUMMER CONTEST 2019 AND MONTHLY CONTESTS FOR 2019-2020

The Annual Summer Contest was awarded in August 2019.

The Monthly contests ran September 2019 through May 2020 excluding October due to the Annual Festival. We received between ten to twelve entries for each contest.

Annual Summer Contest 2019

Sponsored by: Leslie Blakeburn/Barbara Blanks/Florence Bruce/Charles K. Firmage/Lori Goetz/Rose Klix
Judged by: Paul Ford
Subject: Any
Form: Any; 40 lines maximum

LOCKRIDGE CEMETERY
—a Narrative Form

Seeing a weathered, handmade wooden sign
publishing the presence of a cemetery, we drove
for curiosity's sake down an unfamiliar, gravel road
winding its way past fields of cotton and corn.
Shaded by large oak and magnolia trees,
an abandoned burial ground sat at road's end,
quietly proving with names and dates
the existence of proud persons now dead.
Varying cuts of stones arranged in clusters appeared
to represent blood kin and by-marriage relations.

A colorfully clad boy Jesus momentarily
misled us to believe that a living Lockridge
still stood among his forebearers.
But no—the statue, oblivious to our intrusion—
had long fixed its rigid gaze upon
the untended grave of a luckless child.
From the ceramic figure's outstretched hands
startled mockingbirds fluttered up
on our approach.

Near an Arkansas town named
for a Southern Civil War hero,
we lingered with the Lockridges and their kin:
the Davidsons, Lukers, Miltons, Moores—
pictured them tasting their tea
or mint juleps in the nearby gazebo.

We poked wild flowers deep
into dusty jelly jars found on the graves,
then emptied our thermos into them.
Reverently, we read aloud names on the stones
and made up stories—happy, tragic, fanciful—
about the families resting quietly and,
we hoped, contentedly there
at Lockridge Family Cemetery.

FLORENCE BRUCE, Memphis, TN

2nd   Ellen La Corte-Ray, Kingsport, TN
3rd   Lori Goetz, Germantown, TN
1 HM   Ann Carolyn Cates, Southaven, MS
2 HM   Dr. Emory D. Jones, Iuka, MS
3 HM   Russell H. Strauss, Memphis, TN

September 2019 Contest

Sponsored/Judged by: Gail Denham
Subject: First Line Contest. Instructions: Begin poem with the first line of a poem by a favorite poet. Make your poem totally different. Credit the poet for the cited first line of their poem.
Form: Any; 30 lines maximum

A TIME FOR DREAMING
—from "Buddha" by Jack Kerouac

I used to sit under the trees and meditate,
watching butterflies float on the breeze.
Papa said I was daydreaming,
there were leaves to rake and corn to hoe.

Watching butterflies float on the breeze,
I thought of emerald pools and lotus flowers.
There were leaves to rake and corn to hoe;
daydreams won't pay the rent.

I thought of emerald pools and lotus flowers.
Papa said,
"Daydreams won't pay the rent,
even Buddha had to eat."

Papa said,
"There's a time for dreaming, a time for plowing,
even Buddha had to eat."
I watched him hoe the corn.

"There's a time for dreaming, a time for plowing,
a time to keep the wolf from the door."
I watched him hoe the corn
as butterflies flew round the roses.

"A time to keep the wolf from the door."
Papa said I was daydreaming.
As butterflies flew round the roses,
I used to sit under the trees and meditate.

CHARLES K. FIRMAGE, Eagle Pass, TX

2nd	Russell H. Strauss, Memphis, TN
3rd	Florence Bruce, Memphis, TN
1 HM	Rose Klix, Johnson City, TN
2 HM	Dr. Emory D. Jones, Iuka, MS
3 HM	Barbara Blanks, Garland, TX

November 2019 Contest

Sponsored by: PST-Knoxville
Judged by: Connie Jordan Green
Subject: It's all relative or 2 or more related things
Form: Any; 25 lines maximum

A REASON TO STUDY ENGINEERING

In a hot, stuffy classroom
my young brain warped,
struggling to comprehend
the space-time continuum.
At 21, the basic principles
of general relativity
escaped my gravitational field.
My thoughts could bend
around other topics—
calculus, fluid flow—
but time dilation
and gravitational lensing
surpassed
my frame of reference.
Time slowed as my
grade accelerated down;
my brain contracted,
my thought experiment ceased.
I dropped the class,
continuing my studies
in other, hot, stuffy classrooms,
where subjects were,
in my opinion,
relatively easier.

LORI GOETZ, Germantown, TN

2nd   Von S. Bourland, Happy, TX
3rd   Gail Denham, Sunriver, OR
1 HM   Barbara Blanks, Garland, TX
2 HM   Charles K. Firmage, Eagle Pass, TX
3 HM   Sara Gipson, Scott, AR

December 2019 Contest

Sponsored by: JoAn Howerton
Co-Judged by: JoAn Howerton and
Crystal Robbins Czerwinski
Subject: Memories of Christmas
Form: Shakespearean Sonnet

DECEMBER GRIEF

The Christmas after Mama died was sad.
We put out just a few bright, festive things—
no tree, a wreath or two, for we felt bad,
and dinner was just burgers, onion rings.
Nobody tried to bake a pie or bird.
Somebody set the table: habit's thing.
We sat around, but hardly spoke a word,
for what could anybody say or bring
to give us back the presence that we lacked?
Nobody could replace her, no one tried.
Hard as it was, we had to face the fact
that just at Christmas time our mom had died.

So merry Christmas didn't come that year,
but later we revived our Christmas cheer.

FLORENCE BRUCE, Memphis, TN

2nd   Russell H. Strauss, Memphis, TN
3rd   Monty Payne, Bartlett, TN
1 HM   Ann Carolyn Cates, Southaven, MS
2 HM   Sara Gipson, Scott, AR

January 2020 Contest

Sponsored/Judged by: Florence Bruce
Subject: Any
Form: Pantoum; 36 lines maximum

THE RENTERS

The crows passed judgment from the roof,
returning for the winter,
their hoarse music echoing loudly
unnerving the neighbors.

Returning for the winter
they moved into the empty house,
unnerving the neighbors,
wearing black clothes and leather chokers.

They moved into the empty house,
glad to be done touring.
Wearing black clothes and leather chokers—
it felt natural after so many years.

Glad to be done touring,
they were happy to come back to this house—
it felt natural after so many years,
even if the neighbors were stand-offish.

They were happy to come back to this house:
they could write and record all winter long—
even if the neighbors were stand-offish,
their dead-end rental felt like home.

They could write and record all winter long
in a stripped-down, bare-bones house.
Their dead-end rental felt like home:
they played hard rock for the crows and gators.

In a stripped-down, bare-bones house,
their hoarse music echoing loudly,
they played hard rock for the crows and gators.
The crows passed judgment from the roof.

LORI GOETZ, Germantown, TN

2nd   Russell H. Strauss, Memphis, TN
3rd   Barbara Blanks, Garland, TX
1 HM   Mark Hudson, Evanston, IL

February Contest

Sponsored/Judged by: Russell H. Strauss
Subject: Keep Your Sunny Side Up (A humorous poem or a poem about humor)
Form: Any; 40 lines maximum

BEAUTIFUL BACON

Tired of brooding about breeding,
she read self-help books,
and consulted the barnyard shrink.
Days long and dreary, deep in a midlife crisis,
she wanted change.
Color was her declaration of independence,
rebellion via the cosmetic counter.
Burgundy boosted her mood.
She looked fabulous in fuchsia
and vivacious in ruby reds.
The change earned her double-takes,
a few animal growls,
and long, dumb-founded stares:
she walked tall and held her head high.
But alas, no hot dates:
the sty remained the sty;
it was the same old slop for dinner.
Worse still, she could smell it—
they had started the smoker.
She learned the hard way:
you can't put lipstick on a pig.

LORI GOETZ, Germantown, TN

2nd   Jonathan Bennett, Lakeland, TN
3rd   Barbara Blanks, Garland, TX
1 HM Gail Denham, Sunriver, OR

March Contest

Sponsored/Judged by: Lori Goetz
Subject: Yellow
Form: Free Verse; 20 lines maximum

TAUNT

"Yellow" stings me.
It should be a warning,
like the golden stripe on a bee's back,
but I am a lad of ten
and know how words can color opinion.
Call me, "Yellow," and I will dangle
from the limb of the garden oak
or fight the schoolyard bully.
I can never allow you to paint me
in a cowardly hue.
You can tint me "true blue"
or catch me "red handed" in my villainy,
but, even when fear churns
inside me like butter,
I cannot bear for your mocking voice
to splash "Yellow" on my reputation.

RUSSELL H. STRAUSS, Memphis, TN

2nd Von S. Bourland, Happy, TX
3rd Barbara Blanks, Garland, TX
1 HM Monty Payne, Bartlett, TN

April 2020 Contest

Sponsored by: PST-NE
Judged by: Rose Klix
Subject: Any
Form: Any; 40 lines maximum

RECALLING THE TROLLEY

Back in the 1940s,
some thought it was great folly
for any modern passenger
to travel on the trolley,
but as a lad I loved to soar
along the humming track.
I never cared how long I rode
or when I might get back.
The motorman would tip his hat
and give the wheel a spin.
The movement stirred a gentle breeze
to tickle all within,
but city fathers, eager
for modern transportation
ripped up the tracks in an attempt
to counteract stagnation;
so, a bus soon traveled down our street.
Its muffler tiger-roared
and carbon monoxide wafted
as riders climbed aboard.
Folks thought the bus more stylish
and found it quite obscene
that any street conveyance
would not use gasoline
but I think the trolley would today
find environmental praise
and downtown trips were much more fun
in my boyhood days.

RUSSELL H. STRAUSS, Memphis, TN

2nd   Sara Gipson, Scott, AR
3rd   Jonathan Bennett, Lakeland, TN
1 HM   William Hill, Southaven, MS
2 HM   Mark Hudson, Evanston, IL
3 HM   James (Mac) Perry, Brownsville, TN

May 2020 Contest

Sponsored/Judged by: Howard S. Carman, Jr.
Subject: Science; any field
Form: Rhymed; 40 lines maximum

OH, MUSE!

Oh, Muse!
Oh, Urania!
What havoc have we wrecked?
With predictive models
and flattened curves
and guidance so oblique?

Oh, Woe
Oh, Ignorance
What blessings we forsake
with such vast knowledge
from which to draw
yet unable to see our mistake

Oh, Death
Oh, Mercy
Let it come swiftly and without dread
if science cannot save us
let us be ignorant
until we are dead

PAMELA WATSON, Hendersonville, TN

2nd	Barbara Blanks, Garland, TX
3rd	Russell H. Strauss, Memphis, TN
1 HM	Sara Gipson, Scott, AR
2 HM	Lori Goetz, Germantown, TN

63RD ANNUAL MID-SOUTH POETRY FESTIVAL
OCTOBER 19, 2019
MEMPHIS, TN

THE 2019 MID-SOUTH POETRY FESTIVAL

The 63rd Annual Mid-South Poetry Festival was a great success. The kick-off was held Friday evening, October 18, with a potluck dinner and fellowship gathering at the Days Inn community room. Participants were able to get acquainted with our workshop leader, Budd Powell Mahan. In addition, several participants shared their poetry in an open reading session. Janet Qually read her Poet's Field Day award-winning poem titled *Patterns in Life*.

There were twenty-two attendees at Saturday's all-day festival held on the Southwest Tennessee Community College campus. Budd Powell Mahan presented an outstanding program offering numerous helpful tips for improving one's poetic endeavors. He cautioned against using clichés, and stressed the importance of striving for authenticity, as well as having readers connect with encountered writings.

Budd Powell Mahan served as the 16th, 19th, and 25th President of the Poetry Society of Texas. He was editor of ENCORE, the annual festival winners' anthology published by the National Federation of State Poetry Societies. He focused extensively on student programs in Texas, which won thirteen consecutive first places in the NFSPS Student Award. Formerly a teacher, Mr. Mahan is now an actor in the Dallas area who enjoys participating in speaking seminars and poetry readings. While also winning awards for painting and photography, he admits that his greatest fulfillment comes through writing.

PST's first oral poetry award was presented at the festival. Following lunch, contest winners were announced by Russell H. Strauss for all of the twenty-six 2019 competitions. A special thank you is given to everyone who entered, judged, and/or sponsored various contests. Entries this year arrived from TN, AL, AR, FL, IL, KY, LA, MN, MO, MS, NY, OH, OK, OR, TX, UT, VA, and Ontario, Canada.

The 2019 Contest Chair Lori Goetz reported "Total number of poets who entered the contest—53 (of these, 26 were members, 27 were non-members). We had 25% more poets enter this year, vs. 2018. The total number of poems entered was 712. We had 324 more poems this year, vs. 2018 (45% increase)."

Another special thank you goes out to all those who provided lunch, helped set up the meeting room, gave door prizes, brought visitors and other society members, and greatly facilitated the overall enjoyment that ensued. Also, we sincerely appreciate Marilyn Denington who sponsored the 'Best of the Fest' award in memory of her husband.

We are already looking forward to the 64th Annual Mid-South Poetry Festival to be held in the fall of 2020. We hope more attendees at future festivals will also bring copies of their books to sell.

JoAn HOWERTON
2019 FESTIVAL DIRECTOR

ORAL POETRY CONTEST
October 19, 2019

This year was the first time PST included an oral poetry competition at the Festival.

Fourteen contestants competed by reciting or performing their poems. Festival attendees voted for their choices. Janet Qually and Howard S. Carman, Jr. facilitated the judging.

Winners:
1st   Sydney McKissack, Southaven, MS
2nd Luke Richards, Cordova, TN
3rd   Pete Harris, Memphis, TN

WINNERS OF THE FESTIVAL POEMS
OCTOBER 19, 2019

BEST OF THE FEST AWARDED TO BETH STAAS FOR #13, *FINAL WORDS*

Notes:
   The poems have been inserted as near to the poets' original entries as possible. However, when any poem lines extended beyond the margins, adjustments were made to fit the space.

   If curious about specific forms, PST recommends you consult Florence Bruce's Blogspot at http://poemsamples.blogspot.com/ Enter the form name in the search box at the top left of the site. Read the form specifics and at least one example.

Tennessee Voices Anthology

#1 Benefactor's Award

55 entries received
A PST Members-Only Contest—
Poets were allowed to enter any number of poems.
Sponsored by: Anonymous Donors
Judged by: Jerry Hardesty
Subject: Any
Form: Any; 40 lines maximum

THREE UNKNOWNS

I was condensation of contentment
until winds of creation
took me into my mother's womb
where I became form and grew, then pushed
that hyperbolic turn toward death;
with birth's brilliant chill, I shrieked.
Everything so new now;
before is gone, left in the womb
or veiled behind *Deja vu*. My past,
Unknown.

My mathematical mind says
I will never touch the asymptote of death.
In youth, I craved the thrill of closeness,
approaching tangentially but never intersecting.
Older, I take care of myself, for I have seen others
cross that axis, some young, most old.
But each life has its own equation
and I pray mine travels parallel a bit further.
The thought of extinguishing the me I know,
Unknown.

Now my hair is white,
my skin is thin with bruise tattoos.
I hurt as much as I don't.
I continue to scribble nonsense lines
that few will see and fewer read

for my mind says I'm an asymptote,
only approaching death
while my body cries for its touch.
Not now I say, I have one more to write, don't I?
Unknown.

HARVEY STONE, Johnson City, TN

2nd	Dr. Emory D. Jones, Iuka, MS
3rd	Florence Bruce, Memphis, TN
4th	Russell H. Strauss, Memphis, TN
5th	Florence Bruce, Memphis, TN
1 HM	Florence Bruce, Memphis, TN

#2 Poet's Field Day Award

62 entries received
A PST Members-Only Contest—Poets were allowed to enter any number of poems including previously published ones. However, if published, the winning entry is not reprinted in Tennessee Voices.
Sponsored by: Anonymous Donors
Judged by: Dr. Diane Clark
Subject: Any
Form: Any; 40 lines maximum

PATTERNS IN LIFE

This poem was previously posted for members on a website for writers.

JANET QUALLY, Memphis, TN

2nd	Dr. Emory D. Jones, Iuka, MS
3rd	Florence Bruce, Memphis, TN
1 HM	Fay Guinn, Jonesboro, AR
2 HM	Barbara Blanks, Garland, TX
3 HM	Nick Sweet, Shepherd, TX

The Poetry Society of Tennessee

#3 Dr. Wanda Rider Memorial Award

25 entries received
Sponsored/Judged by: Marilyn Denington
Subject: International Travel
Form: Free Verse; 20-30 lines maximum

LEVELER
   —after *Toilets of the World* by Morna E. Gregory and Sian James

Bowing to the deities of bodily function
    and the privilege of solitary relief
with push, pull, twist, crank, flush or stomp
    we all discard that which comes forth.

In crescent moonlight of a Tennessee outhouse
    or before a frescoed urinal in a Wisconsin museum.
In Hong Kong's 14 karat gold bathroom
    or *l'urinette* in Montreal's Whiskey Cafe.

Back-lit glass walls in Johannesburg's Kilimanjaro Nightclub,
    London's pop-up urinal rising from its manhole cover like a god.
From the trunk of a dried cactus in Bolivia's salt desert,
    under a weathered handprinted *baño* sign

where scant pesos are collected for a family's basic needs.
    Count your rubles for a public loo in Moscow,
spend thin air at a stone commode, stoic in the High Andes.
    In Germany or France, a *klofrau* or *madame pipi* may assist you;

Japan could pamper you with heated seats, water jets, then dryers
    to blow you clean.
    Double billings of *weewee* or *doodoo* flushes, curry-scented
pink tents or a campfire's nearby pee tree.
    Crouch over a hole with two footprints like porcelain quotation marks,

aim at dodging fish or painted bees.
    Australia's *dunnies* & *longdrops* inventoried for a National Toilet Map.
Iceland's no-squatting-man signs for cemeteries at the mercy
    of tourists rudely carefree.

Shallow indents by the side of dirt roads, or on ocean lips
    impoverished rows of rickety huts on stilts—
our toilets tell their tales of us,
    & our drowsy tolerance that disregards full

global access to running water on a planet spoiling with dysentery
& cholera until nature calls us   all to our knees.

RIKKI SANTER, Columbus, OH

2nd	Budd Powell Mahan, Dallas, TX
3rd	Howard S. Carman, Jr., Blountville, TN
1 HM	Barbara Funke, Saint George, UT
2 HM	Robert Blenheim, Daytona Beach, FL
3 HM	Barbara Blanks, Garland, TX

#4 Unrequited Contest

34 entries received
Sponsored/Judged by: Bill Howerton
Subject: Love Unrequited
Form: Free Verse; 8-32 lines maximum

REMEMBERING

I catch some evening breezes
trailing down the narrow streets,
echoing your face
coming towards me in the twilight.
Your eyes always reminded me
of windows
open to the depths of our passion.
We loved those nights
into the soft hands of the moon.
That's what I remember.

Parts of you are dangling
around the edges of my life.
My fingertips constantly touch
those framed pictures,
those matched flowers,
those rhymed poems
that quietly whisper your name
in the staggered paths of night.
That's what I remember.

I have my tears to soften
all hurts
and smooth over rough spots remaining.
In the prints of my steps
another world will circle around me
and breathe your memory away.

You have forced my love for you
to wander into space with wings
unattached to any orbit.
That's what I will remember.

CATHERINE MORAN, Little Rock, AR

2nd   Charles K. Firmage, Eagle Pass, TX
3rd   John Ottley, Jr., Alpharetta, GA
1 HM   Lori Goetz, Germantown, TN
2 HM   Florence Bruce, Memphis, TN
3 HM   Harvey Stone, Johnson City, TN

#5 PST-NE Chapter Prize

40 entries received
Sponsored by: PST-NE
Judged by: Shuly Xochitl Cawood
Subject: Any
Form: Any; 50 lines maximum

COMMON ANCESTRY
—after Lisel Muller

1) In 1921, Marie Brunner Healy recorded in her diary
how she'd cast her first ballot and, in a separate entry,
the birth of Mary Coletta, my mother.

2) I was my father's last hope for a boy.

3) I wrote a sentence. Then I wrote another. And so on.

4) At twelve years old, I asked the parish priest,
"How can you be happy in heaven when someone you love is in hell?"
Labeled a heretic, I was freed to invent my own religion.

5) I learned dating as an Olympic sport.

6) The history of the War in Viet Nam coincided perfectly
with the War to save my self-esteem. Both ended rather badly.

7) I knew I was in love when I could sleep through the night.

8) One day, against my father's wishes, I
became a lawyer. Clients' stories changed me.

9) Betty Friedan killed more than one relationship.

10) Mountains, it turns out, are deeper than poetry.

11) In Ireland are many people who look much like my grandfather.
None look like my brown-skinned daughter.

12) Every day for twenty years I've had to ask how best
to love her. Some days that leaves time for nothing else.

13) On 9/11, while I searched the wreckage for words,
my nine-year-old linked arms with our two dogs and sang
We Shall Overcome.

14) After so many years, we are still friends, I say to Donna,
Sherry, Helen, Virginia, Kathy, Margaret, Susan.
I do not say this to my five sisters.

15) *ad infinitum*
In 1969, I watched a man walk on the moon. I thought
I could do that, too.

Eight years later, my father died.
Another eight years later, my mother died.
Another eight years later, my daughter was born.

They come, they go, she carries their names, our ancestry.

NANCY COOK, Saint Paul, MN

2nd	Howard S. Carman, Jr., Blountville, TN
3rd	Lori Goetz, Germantown, TN
1 HM	Gail Denham, Sunriver, OR
2 HM	Dena Gorrell, Edmond, OK
3 HM	Barbara Funke, Saint George, UT
4 HM	Barbara Blanks, Garland, TX

#6 On a Deceased Favorite Poet

26 entries received
Sponsored/Judged by: William Huettel
Subject: A Deceased Poet
Form: Any; 20-40 lines maximum

RENDEZVOUS POET

> —"I have a rendezvous with Death at midnight in some flaming town." Alan Seeger

We each have a rendezvous with death, Alan Seeger,
but many of us manage to postpone
our appointment with that hag
until the waning moments of a long life,
but you were a sensitive youth living abroad
who dreamed of becoming a savior to democracy
and then writing verse about your victory;
so, you joined the French Foreign Legion
before your own country ever went to war.
You were not the first poet to grasp the reality—
of pestilential trenches, swirling bullets,
clouds of poison gas.
Poetic death became international in that conflict,
claiming Britain's Rupert Brooks,
who died of sepsis, far from the land he extolled
aboard a hospital ship in Turkey
and Canada's John McCrae, who wrote of Flanders Fields
only to die of pneumonia
in the military hospital he commanded,
but you, our American poetic sacrifice to that Great War,
died bravely, still cheering the triumph of your fellows
while you lay mortally wounded
in the Battle of the Somme.
The pen, deemed mightier than the sword,
can still fall useless from the hand
from the strike of a single bullet.

How sad that your premature rendezvous
stilled your own pen forever.

RUSSELL H. STRAUSS, Memphis, TN

2nd   Budd Powell Mahan, Dallas, TX
3rd   Mark Hudson, Evanston, IL

#7 Rose Klix Award

35 entries received
Sponsored by: Howard S. Carman, Jr.
Co-Judged by: Howard S. Carman, Jr. & Benjamin A. Dugger
Subject: Faith
Form: Any; 40 lines maximum

THE QUILTERS

We women cut a fabric swatch from clothes
of husbands, brothers, fathers, sons—our men
who died. Though we are bent beneath the blows
of loss, we pick up needles once again
and gather in a circle, quilt the squares,
embroidering their names and dates, then speak
about the ones we loved and raised. Our prayers
are brief for we are strong. We *can't* be weak.
We know our men cannot stay home, but must
go off to fight or work—might not come back—
while we remain at home and soon adjust.
We do what must be done. Life cuts no slack.
    Our faith is strong because when men are gone—
    they often are—we know we must go on.

BARBARA BLANKS, Garland, TX

2nd   Nancy Cook, Saint Paul, MN
3rd   Catherine L'Herisson, Garland, TX

#8 Connections Award

31 entries received
Sponsored/Judged by: Bill Howerton
Subject: Connections
Form: Any; 5-25 lines maximum

AT THE LAKE

I pull sunlight from your hair
to make our shadows pour
to the ground,
where rivulets spill back
to the time we met.

Leaves brush the colors
of secrets barely whispered—
words beyond flight
and dream, strung to
neither root nor bone,
words tumbling in shapes
we've never seen before.

We unbutton the hours
until day and night
meet briefly at the horizon;
they kiss, still making
each other blush
after so many years.

PATTY DICKSON PIECZKA, Carbondale, IL

2nd   Robert Blenheim, Daytona Beach, FL
3rd   Becky Alexander, Cambridge, Ontario, Canada
1 HM   Fay Guinn, Jonesboro, AR

#9 Citizens' Climate Lobby Challenge

20 entries received
Sponsored by: Citizens' Climate Lobby of Northeast TN
Judged by: Dennis Patton
Subject: Climate Change
Form: Any; 12-40 lines

A GLOBAL WARMING COST

The Earth is growing warmer, icy sheets
on polar caps are melting, raising seas
and rubber boots from ankle-heights to knees
for sloshing home from work in rainy streets.

They say the warmer climate causes swings
from cold to hot become intensified
and form the fingers pulling triggers tied
to frequent stormy weather blasting springs.

They say that growing warmer brings more frost
and blizzards chilling winter days below
the freezing mark; but how, I want to know.
I'm sure the science true, though logic's lost.

They say the Earth is warmer, yet I feel
a winter freeze assaulting spring with zeal.

SARA GIPSON, Scott, AR

2nd	Jonathan Bennett, Lakeland, TN
3rd	Rita Moritz, Pell City, AL
1 HM	Fay Guinn, Jonesboro, AR
2 HM	Becky Alexander, Cambridge, Ontario, Canada

#10 John R Benish Memorial Award

19 entries received; Sponsored/Judged by: Dr. Diane Clark
Subject: Gloves (singular or plural)
Form: Any; 20-40 lines

RICH GLOVES–POOR MITTENS

Rich people live in gloves,
the condoms of digits, separate units
like neighbors in a condo complex,
each keeps to its own; no shared warmth.
Specialty and independence is key,
driving, skiing, golfing, football,
leather of course. Living their dream.

Poor folk live in mittens,
the commune of fingers
working as a team, squeezing, holding,
staying warm together.
Living like immigrant families,
sharing sweat and scents.
Teamwork and family.

Do the frostbitten leather families
with their segregation and independence
breathe a better life
than the warm knitted families
huddled together side by side?
Remember: The meek shall inherit the earth
and they make better snowballs.

HARVEY STONE, Johnson City, TN

2nd	Budd Powell Mahan, Dallas, TX
3rd	Gail Denham, Sunriver, OR
1 HM	Christine Riddle, Foley, AL
2 HM	Charles K. Firmage, Eagle Pass, TX
3 HM	Tanya Russell Whitney, Sorrento, LA

#11 Winklebleck Challenge Award

20 entries received
Sponsored/Judged by: Barbara Blanks
Subject: Any
Form: Sonnet; 14-15 lines maximum

A MEASURE OF SHEDDING

My skin is sloughing off throughout the year,
so I remain on leaves and apple stems
along the paths we walked. And I endear
you now with parts of me left on your limbs
and lips like seraphs guarding every door.
I want to be a snake who loses skin
at once and crawls out glistening before
all promises. I'd wrap around you then
and offer all ripe garden fruits. My touch
as fresh as new-found grace is but the edge
of all the wonderings desired so much
as we stand poised upon a fragile ledge.
The good and less-good knowledge of these tales
are measured on those equal garden scales.

CATHERINE MORAN, Little Rock, AR

2nd	Russell H. Strauss, Memphis, TN
3rd	Von S. Bourland, Happy, TX
1 HM	Dennis Patton, Alexander, AR
2 HM	Budd Powell Mahan, Dallas, TX
3 HM	Robert Blenheim, Daytona Beach, FL

#12 In Honor of my 11 Grandchildren
Whose Love Is Unconditional

31 entries received
Sponsored/Judged by: JoAn Howerton
Subject: Generation to Generation
Form: Any; 40 lines maximum

PLOW DEEP THROUGH THAT FOG
—to paraphrase author James Lee Burke: "Age is a separate country that you don't try to explain to young people."

I cannot explain how it is to be old. No one would
understand—especially flighty youngsters who amble
everywhere with earphones carving music lines into
their brain, and fingers that fly over tiny keys, alerting
their friends to mall sales, who did what to
whom—even if that friend sits across the table.

No, they'd tune me out after our first words; glue
their eyes and fingers to small machines, play games
where colorful figures jump from one level
to the next, then explode in a star flash.

Only we who own our six or seven decades of jobs—
children, responsibilities, hassles, grief, dodging from
one crisis to another, building memories—can feel it.

Wind blows straight through from generation to generation.
It tickles the young with dreams of what could be. As I age,
the breezes often chill, carry fear of what's always there,
waiting like incoming tide. However, often my brow
is touched by the sweet breeze of good-time memories.

Memories are what we, the oldsters, hold dear
and what our young are now living,
but do not fully appreciate.
We don't expect immortality;
perhaps faint respect and love.

GAIL DENHAM, Sunriver, OR

2nd	Linda Hoagland, North Tazewell, VA
3rd	Russell H. Strauss, Memphis, TN
1 HM	Fay Guinn, Jonesboro, AR
2 HM	Jeanine Mah, Memphis, TN
3 HM	Curt Vevang, Palatine, IL

#13 Letting Go Award

34 entries received
Sponsored/Judged by: Von S. Bourland
Subject: Letting Go
Form: Any; 16-32 lines maximum

FINAL WORDS

Forgive me, son,
for steering you toward my wants
to read Thoreau and Longfellow,
while you squirmed to be my little man.

Forgive the hours of practice
assuming your passion the same as mine,
a rapture beyond Schubert or Brahms
that vibrates the heavens with their sound.

Forgive my patriot's fervor,
the crisp salutes and rat-a-tat of guns,
as you abandoned this life in favor of war,
a hero in the making

without a chance to learn who you were,
never feeling the sweet gasp
that said it was just a pose
and you really belonged to yourself.

BETH STAAS, Oak Brook, IL

2nd	Patty Dickson Pieczka, Carbondale, IL
3rd	Tanya Russell Whitney, Sorrento, LA
1 HM	Charles K. Firmage, Eagle Pass, TX
2 HM	Frances Cowden, Memphis, TN
3 HM	Rita Moritz, Pell City, AL

#14 The Undercover Contest

37 entries received
Sponsored by: Anonymous Donor
Judged by: Nancy Baass
Subject: Any
Form: Any; 40 lines maximum

WHEN THE LIGHT GOES

A mother calls her children in from play
when light is slowly going from the sky.
She wants them close to her at end of day.
She wants them safely home when shadows fly.

When light is slowly going from the sky,
the children long to linger for a while.
She wants them safely home when shadows fly.
She waits at home to greet them with a smile.

The children long to linger for a while.
Their games are filled with fun and friends are dear.
She waits at home to greet them with a smile.
They say their fond farewells and disappear.

Their games are filled with fun and friends are dear,
but they must now depart as night comes on.
They say their fond farewells and disappear.
The playground seems forlorn when they are gone.

But they must now depart when night comes on.
The darkness has not caught them unaware.
The playground seems forlorn when they are gone.
They hurry home for love is always there.

The darkness has not caught them unaware.
She wants them close to her at end of day.
They hurry home, for love is always there.
A mother calls her children in from play.

LaVERN SPENCER McCARTHY, Blair, OK

2nd	Janet Qually, Memphis, TN
3rd	Curt Vevang, Palatine, IL
1 HM	Linda Hoagland, North Tazewell, VA
2 HM	John Ottley, Jr., Alpharetta, GA
3 HM	Dr. Emory D. Jones, Iuka, MS

#15 Try Something New Award

19 entries received
Sponsored/Judged by: Lori Goetz
Subject: Any
Form: Haibun or Tanka Prose; 30 lines maximum

EXCERPTS FROM A NISELI DIARY, 1942

Mrs. Inouye fans against the oppressive heat with a paper fan as some ancestral matron might have done in the days of the shoguns. We have come to the desert. The tar paper huts of the Manzanar Relocation Center look like lumps of rice sitting in a granite bowl of mountains. Rocks beat like machine gun pellets against the tires of our bus. Before father left Frisco, he tacked above the door of our grocery the only flag to which he had ever sworn allegiance. He sighed at its bold stars and stripes, then taped to the door a sign reading, "I am an American."

> This blazing red orb,
> much like Japan's rising sun,
> is scorching our souls.

Our school has no lab equipment and few books, but we must continue to learn. No need to complain! Our elders say *Shikata ga nai.* I understand little of my ancestral tongue, but it seems to mean, *It cannot be helped.* Our Boy Scouts recently held a ceremony honoring Nisei soldiers who have died defending our nation against the Nazis. Do they not understand where our hearts lie? The sixty students that share our classroom pledge allegiance every morning, declaring there is "liberty and justice for all."

> American dream?
> Buzzards circle above, wait
> to feed on our hopes.

There are twenty people in a room for four. Even a coyote can sometimes drift from the pack to find privacy. Mr. Roosevelt, who once said, "The only thing we have to fear is fear itself." We have been law-abiding in this land. Why do you fear us?

> My imprisoned heart
> longs to float like an eagle,
> freely in the breeze.

RUSSELL H. STRAUSS, Memphis, TN

2nd	Janet Qually, Memphis, TN
3rd	Barbara Funke, Saint George, UT
1 HM	Nancy Cook, St. Paul, MN
2 HM	Sara Gipson, Scott, AR
3 HM	Dr. Emory D. Jones, Iuka, MS

#16 Pat Smith Memorial Award

15 entries received
Sponsored/Judged by: Florence Bruce
Subject: Any
Form: Blank Verse; 20-40 lines maximum

FLIGHT TO DAKOTA

—"I have always said that I would never have been President had it not been for my experience in North Dakota."
Theodore Roosevelt

I left my infant daughter with her aunt.
I had no heart for caring for her then.
I lived with rattlesnakes and meadowlarks.
The Badlands are no different than those
that others foolishly do not call, "Bad,"
and harbor both their own adversities
and those amenities that strengthen souls.
In February 1884,
my mother died of typhoid in my home
and, on that self-same day in that same house,
my wife, whose name I shall no longer speak,
for silence tends to dull the blades of grief,
died two days after having birthed a child.
I wrote into my diary that day
these words, "The light has gone out of my life."
I once had been a weak and sickly lad
but through determination I had honed
my body; yet new strength would be required.
I needed now to hone my grieving soul;
so, fleeing from New York, I took a train
across an endless stretch of grass and sky
to open a Dakota cattle ranch
with no man to rely on but myself.
I do declare it was a healthy life.
I hunted, herded, hewed my cabin logs.
A wayward river cut through cottonwood
and here I dwelt within its sigmoid curve.

At silent dusk, when all my chores were done,
I watched the strangely God-misshapen buttes
turn purple in the sunset afterglow.
I read my books and rocked and learned to heal.
In '87, deadly winter cold
destroyed my herd, but now I carry home
determination to conserve a land
where nature tests the man whose spirit flags
to strengthen his resolve and set it free.

RUSSELL H. STRAUSS, Memphis, TN

1 HM   Janet Qually, Memphis, TN

#17 Bobbie Drobeck Award

20 entries received
Sponsored/Judged by: Russell H. Strauss
Subject: Reference one of these popular drinks: beer, wine, coffee, tea, or carbonated beverages
Form: Narrative Poem; 10-40 lines maximum

THE KNIGHT'S QUEST

Amid the flash of lightning bolts against the darkened sky
A horseman clad in silver scales went stoutly riding by.
A knight of yore with polished sword encased in jeweled sheath;
A posture formed of brave resolve one would with joy bequeath.
For many days he knew the sound of thumping hoofs on stone;
But many years he knew the pain that found himself alone.

Much time elapsed as goodly knight rode over many lands
And drank his mead in places no sun beamed its warming hands.
He rode through many thickened woods and crossed infected plains,
Stepping over chasms deep and passing men's remains.
Then finally came, one fateful day, upon a place of rest:
A sacred stream that signified the ending of his quest.

Across the river on the bank a startling figure stood:
A glowing girl in flimsy garb, a gypsy of the wood.
Her limbs adorned with bracelets gold, her body wrapped in silk.
Beyond the garments and the gold her skin was white as milk.
So bravely he stepped off the bank into the water's flow
And headed toward the other side while feeling passion grow.

He fought his chainmail's clutching weight, persisting in his crossing
As in his mind some haunted dreams of his desires were tossing.
She smiled and beckoned, leading him into her soothing arms,
Bestowing mollifying solace with some other charms,
And wrapped his scales with golden rings, circles magnetized;
But the moment that his lips touched hers, the vision vaporized.

The knight in water floundered only inches from the bank.
She cried and stretched her fingers out to give his hand a yank.
Their hands just touched a second then were disengaged in space

But to him it never mattered for the knight had seen her face.
Whatever he had seen there was the last he saw that night.
The water closed about him and he disappeared from sight. . .

The gypsy of the wood remains beside the river bank.
She sits serene and silent for the multitudes that sank.
It is known that no knights reached her; it is not known if one will.
But her tears have made the river, and the river's never still.
Now winter's here and all has froze, o'er land a stillness creeps.
And though the knights have ceased to come, a vigil still she keeps.

ROBERT E. BLENHEIM, Daytona Beach, FL

2nd	Becky Alexander, Cambridge, Ontario, Canada
3rd	Barbara Blanks, Garland, TX
1 HM	LaVern Spencer McCarthy, OK
2 HM	Jerri Hardesty, Brierfield, AL
3 HM	Rita Moritz, Pell City, AL

#18 Family Ties Award

29 entries received
Sponsored by: Anna's Pet Sitting
Judged by: Gail Denham
Subject: Family
Form: Any; 4-20 lines maximum

PHONING MY SISTER

I call each day.
Sometimes her husband answers
and we discuss lab results, biopsy reports, discharge plans.
Sometimes it's my niece or nephew, and I can hear fear
poking holes through their faith in God's inclination to answer
  prayer.
But today my sister picks up and I hear
the ragged edge that used to be her sweet voice.
So, I do most of the talking, tethering her
to what used to be her day to day, to what persists
despite her absence from it.
My sister loves birds, so I save the best for last.
"This morning," I tell her, "I watched a flock of grackles
taking a communal shower under the lawn sprinkler in the
  garden."
She chuckles, and I imagine her smile.
And that's why, for as long as it takes,
I call each day.

CHRISTINE RIDDLE, Foley, AL

2nd   Barbara Blanks, Garland, TX
3rd   John Ottley, Jr., Alpharetta, GA
1 HM   Rita Moritz, Pell City, AL
2 HM   Janice Hoffman, Williamsburg, VA
3 HM   Florence Bruce, Memphis, TN

#19 In Memory of Jo Elliott

25 entries received
Sponsored/Judged by: Pete Harris
Subject: Any
Form: Limerick; 5 lines

SCRABBLED

I once liked a game with word tiles,
that promised me chuckles and smiles,
But the 'Z' and the 'Q'
only ever came through
when no vowels were left in my pile!

BECKY ALEXANDER,
Cambridge, Ontario, Canada

2nd	Barbara Blanks, Garland, TX
3rd	Florence Bruce, Memphis, TN
1 HM	Budd Powell Mahan, Dallas, TX
2 HM	Fay Guinn, Jonesboro, AR
3 HM	Howard S. Carman, Jr., Blountville, TN

The Poetry Society of Tennessee

#20 PST-Knoxville Award

22 entries received
Sponsored by: PST-Knoxville
Judged by: Ann Thornfield Long
Subject: Bridges (any interpretation)
Form: Any; 25-40 lines maximum

BEWITCHED

I stood bewitched beneath the Three Oaks Bridge
and heard you sing *Sweet Dreams* above my head.
A soft chill grew, although September sun
was warm against the stone that spanned the bed.

My ankles blushed beneath the water's rush
in frozen movement to conceal the rude
intrusion of an unintended breach,
an eavesdrop that would sabotage the mood.

That day became a cherished secret held
untold, as I rehearsed my own sweet dream,
pursuing till the walls of will came down,
until I had forgotten bridge and stream.

Today, *Sweet Dreams* comes clear from laundry's whip
and I recant that I forgot the past,
as voice and lyric hang the clothesline pole
remind when music charmed and fates were cast.

All practiced lines inadequately tell
the story of a song sung from above
that lured, as Lorelei in ancient tale,
a heart to the abandonment of love.

And so the saga comes into your ear
as I relate a boy caught in a spell
who stood in shadows of the Three Oaks Field
and knew desire that time would never quell.

With dishes done, the sun completely set,
the porch swing creaks accompany your lilt
and we are once again at Three Oaks Creek
the sword of song inserted to the hilt.

BUDD POWELL MAHAN, Dallas, TX

2nd	Janet Qually, Memphis, TN
3rd	Russell H. Strauss, Memphis, TN
1 HM	Robert Blenheim, Daytona Beach, FL
2 HM	Gail Denham, Sunriver, OR

#21 Dorsimbra Contest

11 entries received
Sponsored by: JoAn Howerton
Judged by: Crystal Robbins Czerwinski
Subject: Family traditions
Form: Dorsimbra

NIGHTS IN THE SWAMP

Swept into the dust bins of history,
gone are the magic chants of witch doctors.
At night I hear the swamp whisper to me;
Mama says I had better stay indoors.

Papa poles
a pirogue,
hunts gators
while the moon shines.

Mama tells me a bad moon is rising,
sets the candles bought from Billie Bess
next to Mary, because magic has been
swept into the dust bins of history.

CHARLES K. FIRMAGE, Eagle Pass, TX

2nd   Jonathan Bennett, Lakeland, TN
3rd   Barbara Blanks, Garland, TX
1 HM   Russell H. Strauss, Memphis, TN
2 HM   Jerri Hardesty, Brierfield, AL
3 HM   Frances Cowden, Memphis, TN

#22 Joan T. and Sheron B. Strauss Award

15 entries received
Sponsored/Judged by: Russell H. Strauss
Subject/Form: A classic Burma Shave poem whereby the last line is always BURMA SHAVE

TOO SLOW

Too slow
in the fast lane,
never moved over.
Now in the median
pushing up clover.
BURMA SHAVE

HOWARD S. CARMAN, JR., Blountville, TN

2nd	Rose Klix, Johnson City, TN
3rd	Dena Gorrell, Edmond, OK
1 HM	Sara Gipson, Scott, AR
2 HM	Rita Moritz, Pell City, AL
3 HM	LaVern Spencer McCarthy, Blair, OK

#23 Fibonacci Poem Award

19 entries received
Sponsored/Judged by: Gail Denham
Subject: Any (Humorous)
Form: Fibonacci Poem; 6 lines, 20 syllables

PAMPHLET OFFER FROM MY NEW TELEPHONE FRIEND IN INDIA

> My
> name
> is John.
> I offer
> for twelve ninety-five
> "How to Stop Intrusive Phone Calls."

RUSSELL H. STRAUSS, Memphis, TN

2nd	Rose Klix, Johnson City, TN
3rd	Jonathan Bennett, Lakeland, TN
1 HM	Budd Powell Mahan, Dallas, TX
2 HM	Charles K. Firmage, Eagle Pass, TX
3 HM	Catherine L'Herisson, Garland, TX

#24 Time to Reflect Award

23 entries received
Sponsored/Judged by: Lori Goetz
Subject: Divisions
Form: Free Verse; 10-20 lines maximum

SLOW STEPS

Dread drew a bead on my lungs.
Breath came in gasps.
Twenty-two years since I'd
seen her. It didn't end well.

Now she wants to make things right. Said
she was terminal. My strong opinioned,
careless *Madre* wanted absolution, desired
release for years of abuse and neglect.

The pavement beneath me was dark,
gritty. Ahead, a neon sign blinked
the cafe motto. She'd be there, on the edge
of her chair, like a cat ready to pounce.

My feet dragged. Shoes were soaked through.
Rained all week. Skies as black as my thoughts.
Suddenly I couldn't move. She'd look pitiful, needy,
seeking forgiveness, sympathy—emotions
I could no longer dredge up.

Slowly I turned, retraced soggy steps. Not now.
Not this time. I'd send a letter. We'd talk by phone.
No threat there. I began to run, erased the coffee
shop image. Wanted to hum, but my throat was too dry.

GAIL DENHAM, Sunriver, OR

2nd   Frances Cowden, Memphis, TN
3rd   Jonathan Bennett, Lakeland, TN
1 HM   Barbara Blanks, Garland, TX
2 HM   Russell H. Strauss, Memphis, TN
3 HM   Jerri Hardesty, Brierfield, AL

#25 Personification Contest

26 entries received
Sponsored/Judged by: Florence Bruce
Subject: Any
Form: Any; 40 lines maximum

GOSSIPING HINGES

Some think we hinges only squeak
because we seek
an oily drop
to make us stop,
but hinges gossip day and night,
our message, quite
distinctive. We,
with raucous glee,
say 'hi' to hinges down the street
we'd like to meet,
or squawk a song
for sing-a-long.

When hinges squall in unison,
our voices run
from shy to bold.
If truth be told,
when doors and shutters bang the house
from wind's carouse,
we hinges will,
with rusty zeal,
be heard in every part of town,
up hill and down,
our sounds like those
of rasping crows.

LaVERN SPENCER McCARTHY, Blair, OK

1 HM Von S. Bourland, Happy, TX

#26 In Memory of Dotty Katz

19 entries received
Sponsored/Judged by: Lynnie Mirvis
Subject: The Color Purple
Form: Any; 20 lines maximum

WALKING WITH MY MOTHER

Deep in wings I can't recall your easy
sway of hips or the rhythm of your heels;
instead there is the plumage of lavender cane,
violet walker, then orchid wheelchair that names you.

Your purples were your feathered campaign.
The folklore of our strolling, me the pusher
you the pushed and the craning of our necks
to meet each other's eyes.

I know in your dreams your legs walked
along beaches, through strange lagoons,
around the rooms of your last home.
Tonight I glide on air currents searching for you

    in the ether until I spot a great morph heron striding
    through her shallows eyes sparkling amethyst in moonlight.

RIKKI SANTER, Columbus, OH

2nd	Catherine Moran, Little Rock, AR
3rd	Harvey Stone, Johnson City, TN
1 HM	Lori Goetz, Germantown, TN
2 HM	Jerri Hardesty, Brierfield, AL
3 HM	Barbara Blanks, Garland, TX
4 HM	Charles K. Firmage, Eagle Pass, TX

STUDENT WINNERS (2019-2020)

Student Contest Coordinator: Frances Cowden

All winners, teachers, and families were invited to the awards Saturday, April 6, 2020 at 2 pm in Colonial Park UMC. First Place poems are published. Other placements are listed below the judge's name, with poet's name, poem title, school, and teacher information.

ELEMENTARY DIVISION (GRADES 2-5)
THE ARCHER

The Archer is aiming
The birds are singing
Up and down, left and right
The arrow is flying

OLIVIER DYLAN SMITH
Snowden Elementary School, Memphis, TN
Teacher: Laura Braytenbah

ELEMENTARY SCHOOL JUDGE: WHITNEY WRIGHT

2nd *Oh Map!,* **Scarlett Niu**, Grahamwood Elementary School, Memphis, TN, Teacher: Sherry Coates
3rd *Spring,* **Paulina Montes**, Shelby Oakes Elementary School, Memphis, TN, Teacher: Amelia Bogdal
4th *Maid to Made,* **Zuleyma Estradra Pena**, Grahamwood Elementary School, Memphis, TN, Teacher: Sherry Coates
HM *Drawing,* **Aydin Rashada**, Shelby Oakes Elementary School, Memphis, TN, Teacher: Amelia Bogdal
HM *Greed,* **Raymond Cui**, Grahamwood Elementary School, Memphis, TN, Teacher: Laura Wilons

JUNIOR DIVISION (GRADES 6 TO 8)
BEDTIME

A time for bed,
A bed for sleep,
Sleep for dreams,
Dreams for thoughts,
Thoughts for feelings,
Feelings for life,
Life for what?
What for?
For time?
Time for the world,
World for the people,
People for change,
Change for time,
Time for what?
Bed?

HAYES BENNETT
White Station Middle School, Memphis, TN
Teacher: Karla Varriano

MIDDLE SCHOOL JUDGE:
RUSSELL H. STRAUSS

2nd *Flame of Anger*, **Savannah Solomon**, West Wilson Middle School, Mt. Juliet, TN, Teacher: Cheryle Scudder
3rd *Realism* **Amy Zhang**, White Station Middle School, Memphis, TN, Teacher: Donna Nanney
4th *Random*, **Kallista Wright**, White Station Middle School, Memphis, TN, Teacher: Donna Nanney
1 HM *Paying No Mind*, **Jerry Xiao**, Memphis University School, Memphis, TN, Teacher: Dax Torrey
2 HM *A Walk in the Woods*, **Eden Holding**, White Station Middle School, Memphis, TN, Teacher: Karla Varriano
3 HM *Sapling*, **Virginia Feng**, White Station Middle School, Memphis, TN, Teacher: Karla Varriano

SENIOR DIVISION (GRADES 9-12)
a lover who hates all

    chocolate, though silky and sweet,
    induces retching and gagging
    only ninety percent cocoa or above will do
    she can only stomach it bitter, dark, and bought by me.

    winter is icy pain in the nose and toes
    spring is the sting of a viscous honeybee
    summer is sweating through her layer of clothes
    she endures autumn, for under falling leaves she met me.

    a baby becomes the trauma of her mother
    nine months agony is the price of pregnancy
    and the result is too easy to ignore or smother
    but she says she'll have one if it's with me.

    to be loved by a lover who hates all but me
    is an empowering and precarious place to be.

ALLISON SCHRANZ
Germantown High School, Germantown, TN
Teacher: Elizabeth Stuart

HIGH SCHOOL JUDGE: LORI GOETZ

2nd *Two New Legs*, **Kayla Murphy**, Germantown High School, Germantown, TN, Teacher: Elizabeth Stuart
3rd *Tickle in My Throat*, **Rebecca Schranz**, Germantown High School, Germantown, TN, Teacher: Elizabeth Stuart
4th *Grandma's Dumpling*, **Amanda Zhou**, White Station High School, Memphis, TN, Teacher: Scott Harrison
HM *At the vulnerable age of thirteen*, **Jada Parker**, Germantown High School, Germantown, TN, Teacher: Elizabeth Stuart
HM *Letter to Red Pond*, **Marissa Liu**, Collierville High School, Collierville, TN, Teacher: Betsy Herlong

EYE POEM PLACEMENTS
JUDGE: WHITNEY BRINKLEY WRIGHT

MIDDLE SCHOOL

2nd *Own Your*, **Audrey Webb**, White Station Middle School, Memphis, TN, Teacher: Donna Nanney
3rd *Rebirth*, **Adele Thompson**, White Station Middle School, Memphis, TN, Teacher: Karla Varriano
4th *How*, **Mollee Long**, White Station Middle School, Memphis, TN, Teacher: Karla Varriano

HIGH SCHOOL

2nd *Still Live*, **DeMarko Reed**, Germantown High School, Germantown, TN, Teacher: Elizabeth Stuart
3rd *Family*, **Luis Negrete**, Germantown High School, Germantown, TN, Teacher: Elizabeth Stuart

THE EYE POEM

The Eye Poem was invented by Kenneth L. Beaudoin (1913-1995), one of the founders of the Poetry Society of Tennessee.

An Eye Poem is created as a poetic collage using visual and verbal imagery. A free verse poem is constructed by combining images from magazine pages with words, phrases and clauses to create a poem on one page. The objective is to create a mood or inspiration. Do not write a poem first and then look for pictures. The poem is a discovery of words that fit with the graphics. You should be able to read the poem three feet away.

Find a picture or pictures up to 8 1/2 x 11 inches. Vertical is best. Go through one or more magazines and find words or phrases etc. that remind you of the graphics (pictures).

Cut the words out neatly and place on the page of graphics. Do not use words smaller than 14 font. LARGE WORDS will be read louder and have more emphasis. Do not cut out letters to make a word.

Position the words and images on the page. If the Eye Poem will be submitted for contests, publication, or will be framed, do not place any words (or crucial parts of an image) close to the paper's edge so that no words or images are cropped during production or publication.

Titles of Eye Poems are the same as the word (or words) in the first line on the page.

The following are this year's First Place winners in the Middle School and High School categories.

ALONE

JONAS MARSHALL
Siegel Middle School, Murfreesboro, TN
Teachers: Sara Adams & Kimberly Risner

SWEET

ALISON SCHRANZ
Germantown High School, Germantown, TN
Teacher: Elizabeth Stout

PATRON POEMS

PST gratefully acknowledges and appreciates the donations from all the Patrons. The following are the Patron Poem selections for 2019-2020.

HOME TO GLORY
—Sand Hill County, South Carolina 1950

Late November,
the weather's still warm
as two scruffy boys shoot
marbles in the front yard,
while Bobby Sue sits
on the steps, playing harmonica.
Mama's in the kitchen fixin'
cornbread. Chickens run
for cover as Thanksgiving looms.
Tomorrow there'll be singing
in church 'bout goin' home
to glory, and listening to the choir.
Bobbie Sue watches
her brothers playing as,
"I Saw the Light," by Hank Williams
comes on the radio. It'll be night
before Papa's shift ends
at the chalk mine. Seems
the only ones goin' home to glory's
these chickens. Papa'll offer
grace, say, "Pass the dumplings
please," and call it good.

CHARLES K. FIRMAGE, Eagle Pass, TX

THE JAPANESE MAPLE

Green leaves
embryonic—
pale, tentative
lacy standards still tightly furled:
growing,
reaching to the sun, spiky crowns
as fragile as paper—
living, breathing
vibrant.

LORI GOETZ, Germantown, TN

THE SPIDER IN THE JUNKYARD
—based on a true story

Back in the long ago Evanston days,
some mischievous children went to play.
In a junkyard, that is no longer there,
they went in an abandoned car on a dare.

They weren't scared to play in the abandoned car,
till a spider appeared, and they ran away far!
A junkyard couldn't scare the kids away,
but a spider kept them from returning to play.

Spiders can scare little girls and even boys;
and keep them out of junkyards in Illinois.
Jim grew up to be a fearless marine;
but ever since then, he has always hated green.

It shows that childhood phobias prove;
when you see a spider, get up and move!

MARK HUDSON, Evanston, IL

LATE OR SOON — QUESTINGS

Ten years, more or less, from the hour of my birth,
Would it make such a change in total worth?
Would there live a stranger within this dusky skin,
Or would I be what I have always been?

Too soon, and would I care less
For the ideas I now profess?
Would I know more the spirit of man,
Or would I struggle under a darker band?

Would I have found a gentle place
To echo all of a people's grace,
Or would my life have been so grim
That I'd not see the love of Him?

Had I been born ten years late,
Would I again have learned to hate
All mankind, my own included?
Would no one be excluded?

Could I walk along and find
Some little good in all mankind,
Or would the world have changed so much,
That not one person would I dare touch?

One decade. . .
Could it affect such drastic change
That I would not know the me that remains?

RUBY J. JONES, Memphis, TN

KING OF THE MOMENT

I am Red-Winged Blackbird,
King of my world,
from bottom to top.
All I touch and see
becomes mine
for this time.
Atop my tree I balance
on its fingertips
to view my salted sky.
I own this moment.
Hear me sing.

ROSE KLIX, Johnson City, TN

In 2005, poem was published in *Schrom Hills Park* chapbook and 2012 in *Pastiche of Poetry, Vol. I*.

EMBRACE

JANET QUALLY, Memphis, TN

SOMEONE TO SHARE THE DYING

Bud Roberts died in a hospice in Bournemouth,
England, July 30, 1998. I was a minister with the
Methodist Church and he was the minister's spouse.
We were married two years. Memories dance in

no particular order. Betty's surprise, a bluebell
carpet in a secluded wood. Carisbrooke Priory
and sweet folks praying for Bud when they knew.
Driving on the wrong side of miniature roads.

Hiking with Bud out in fields on the Isle of Wight,
signs pointing to London and New York City.
Our tiny bedroom by a stream in the granny flat
at the side of Brian and Betty's cottage in Whitwell,

doves cooing over us. The sorrow we denied in order
to live joyfully the time we had (and we did).
Church teas, cold quiche and sausage rolls every time.
Learning to request a proper cuppa tea.

My first funeral in Godshill where I preached from
Genesis to the Cross. My first wedding a joyous occasion
for which the Wroxall folks painted their chapel.
There had not been a wedding there in a long while.

None of these things explains how it is that a
fifty something woman from Tennessee attending
theological school in Atlanta, Georgia, met a man from
South Carolina, both of them longing for a companion;

she for someone with whom to share her new life,
and he, as it turned out unexpectedly,
        for someone to share the dying.

CAROL ROBERTS, Hendersonville, TN

BETWEEN US TWO

    They told me, their good big girl
    that when the baby came
    I would have to help
    and we practiced on my dolls

    this is how you hold the baby
    this is how you support the baby's head
    this is how mommy makes you part of what is happening

    But you,
    you would not consent to be a thing
    passive and docile
    like a baby doll
    waiting where I placed you
    for the tea party to begin

    You were always a feral cat
    a treed raccoon
    hissing and spitting
    your independence at me
    while I blinked my incomprehension
    back at you.

    It wasn't my idea you know.
    Big sister was a foreign concept
    until they told me how it worked
    until they told me what it meant
    that to be a good big sister
    was to be responsible for you

and when it didn't work
when their solution
to sibling rivalry
to petty jealousy
crashed and burned
and we fought like sisters do
they washed their hands
and blamed us
they washed their hands
and left us
to sort it out between us two

PAMELA WATSON, Hendersonville, TN

REPRINTED PATRON POEMS

The following pages contain Patron Poems from the 2018-2019 Tennessee Voices anthology which previously contained publishing errors.

BOY BY THE LAKE
—a day at the Chicago Botanical Garden, May 21, 2012

A robin appears in front of my eyes.
The boy calls to his mother.
He takes a picture of what he sees.
Is it a fish or is it a duck?
A giant swan lazily drifts.
The breeze gently blows on the lake.
The boy photographs his mother.
I sit beneath the shade of the trees.
Snowdrop Anemone hides under the shade.
A seed bud crabapple guards
another bark covered tree.
As other children laugh in the distance,
a spider crawls on my shirt and I kill it.
Like the t-shirt I saw the other day—

We have nothing to fear but
Fear itself and Spiders.
The dead spider's blood is on my hands.
Do I feel Buddhist remorse?
No, the universe is too large
to mourn the loss of a dead spider.
But a good haiku could give
the spider justice and immortality.

      Oh, spider, I knew
   you crossed upon my shirt once.
      I'm sorry you died.

MARK HUDSON, Evanston, IL

Published in the Spring 2018 edition of *Poems of the World*.

MY MUSE SINGS ONLY COUNTRY

My Muse sings only country,
Crying, dying, going somewheres
In a jukebox beat.

I am
Roadhouse Homer
Honkey-Tonk Laureate
Singing to the rhythm
Of roaring engines
And humming tires.

I tease
Tears from
Good ole boys
Where waitresses are Didos
In a cross-country odyssey.

My Muse sings only country.

DR. EMORY D. JONES, Iuka, MS

CALORIE COLLECTION

Calories collect,
but not on my cupboard shelf
or out of sight in the frig.
My stash isn't in my purse
but sits visible to the world:
on my waist, my thighs,
under my arms and chin.
I'm saving, but forgot for what
on which rainy day.
Now it's time to spend
those calories at the gym.

ROSE KLIX, Johnson City, TN

In 2013, poem was published in her chapbook *Eat, Diet, Repeat*.

THE ROAD TAKEN
—after Robert Frost

Shake Paul's right hand while Passing the Peace.
You'll grasp his three straight-cut finger stubs
left by spinning teeth of a Craftsman circular saw.
He'll stare at them as if trying to remember.

Catherine always claimed a pew seat at the back
until with no notice last August. Her Sunday family
sat Friday at 4:00 with two out-of-state cousins.
The casket's grain pattern resembled a rabbit's ear.

Deacon Ron got caught in the third deadly sin.
His wife took tea with her book club as she decided.
His pals bought his coffee and breakfast at Shoney's,
listened under their guy sports' talk—just in case.

Some say the sacred is in nature. They blacken leaves
on lanes bending in undergrowth through choirs
of white trillium under evergreens, worship alone
near a noble oak overlooking a pacific valley. But

another way makes all the difference to me. I reach
into the first century for a foot towel and stoneware
water basin, tuck in extra denarii for a watchful walk
to Jericho on a seldom chosen road with other pilgrims.

Take Paul to see Lowe's shiny John Deere mowers.
Sing "Rock of Ages" with Catherine's downcast kin.
Watch Ron push hash browns around with a fork.
Along this path rise my prayers—and my poems.
(revised 2020)

CALVIN ROSS, Johnson City, TN

ON JOHN LESLIE KOLP'S RETIREMENT

John!
Your life is a wilderness trail we must explore.
Oh, the wonders you have brought forth for earth for all.

John!
You are a flower in a world of weeds,
for people like you, we have great need.

John!
You have planted many seeds.
The trees whose deep roots hug stunning earth keeping dirt
   in its place.
Soon all you have sowed will bud, bloom, grow.

Look!
There goes John trekking wondrous trails.
Hear echoes Italian dolomites, Swiss Alps
sing your praise.

Heard John is in Austria gazing at a total Eclipse.
No, he is in Yosemite now, kicking up dust.
Yesterday, today, tomorrow, he will be refracting the Sun,
whitewashing black tar roofs in the very scorching Sun.
We see John with a hoe in hand.
Oh street steward stopping invading killer species
to save many an urban garden from decay, misery, and rot.

There goes, John!
On the upper westside bicycling to keep the air fresh and clean.
Heard John was in many street protests marching for natural causes.
One thing is for sure when it comes to earth,
John could not resist doing more.

And yes! There is, "No planet B."
Thank Goodness for your trailblazing shining light for saving
us from urban blight.

John!
You have left your mark too numerous to scroll here.
And when you depart this excellent earth,
Old street Steward, John!
We will see you in a natural habitat,
the Sierra Club on the other side

And, yes!
We will sit and chat with George Washington, Abraham Lincoln,
Theodore Roosevelt, and Franklin D. Roosevelt, too.
And, we will talk about the world we once knew.

VINCENT J. TOMEO, Flushing, NY

—written on Amtrak Train No. 195 NW Region to Washington, DC, May 6, 2018

INDEX OF FIRST PLACE WINNERS

Alexander 65
Blanks 48
Blenheim 63
Bruce 20, 25
Carman 69
Cook 45
Denham 54, 71
Firmage 22, 68, 84
Gipson 50
Goetz 23, 27, 28, 85
Hudson 86, 94
Jones, Emory, 95
Jones, Ruby 87
Klix 88, 96
Mah iv
Mahan 67
McCarthy 57, 73
McKissack 35
Moran 43, 52
Pieczka 49
Qually 39, 89
Riddle 64
Roberts 90
Ross 97
Santer 41, 74
Staas 36, 55
Stone 38, 51
Strauss 29, 30, 47, 59, 61, 70
Tomeo 99
Watson 32, 92

Students
Bennett 77
Marshall, 81
Schranz 78, 82
Smith 76